KU-033-852

DAVID LIVINGSTONE

OTHER TITLES IN THE *HEROES OF THE CROSS* SERIES

DAVID
LIVINGSTONE

MARSHALL PICKERING

Marshall Morgan and Scott
Marshall Pickering
34–42 Cleveland Street, London W1P 5FB

Copyright © 1982 Marshall Morgan & Scott
First published by Oliphants Ltd 1953
Reprinted 1954, 1956, 1957, 1960
First issued in paperback in Lakeland 1961
This edition published in 1982 by Marshall Morgan and Scott
Publications Ltd
Part of the Marshall Pickering Holdings Group

Reprinted 1987
89 90: 10 9 8 7 6 5 4
This reissue 1989

All rights reserved. No part of this publication may be repro-
duced, stored in a retrieval system, or transmitted, in any
form or by any means, electronic, mechanical, photocopying,
recording or otherwise, without the prior permission in
writing, of the publisher.

ISBN: 0 551 00942 X

Printed in Great Britain by
Cox & Wyman Ltd, Reading

CONTENTS

AS A BOY

SOME years ago, the minister of a church in Scotland was very disappointed because only one new member had joined the church in a whole year, but that one was David Livingstone, whose name was later to be known all over the world as a missionary hero and a fearless explorer.

As a boy David lived near the banks of a great river in Scotland called the Clyde. I was going to say that David played on the banks of the Clyde; but, when I come to think of it, I must not say that, because I do not think David ever had much time for play. He lived in days, happily gone by, when little boys whose fathers and mothers were not rich were sent to work in factories when they were about seven years of age, and as they worked from early morning until late in the evening and did not have a holiday, even on Saturdays, they could not play very much. David's father and mother were poor people, and they had to put David to work early to help to get bread and butter, and boots and clothes, for his little brothers and sisters. But they were very kind parents, and very good, pious people, who taught their children to love Jesus and to live as He would like us to live. Still, David's father, though he worked hard selling tea in small packets from door to door, did not find it easy to pay the rent of even a little room in Blantyre and keep his boys and girls clothed and fed.

David's other name was Livingstone. Both his father and mother were Scots whose ancestors had lived among the mountains, and been made strong and healthy by working in the open air and eating plenty of simple food. So David was always thankful for his parentage, and when he grew up he was proud that the Livingstones had always been honest, God-fearing people, who could look anybody in the face without needing to be ashamed. And they were brave people, too! One of David's ancestors had died fighting for his king at the battle of Culloden. David's mother brought up her children in the love and fear of God, and his father set them a good example by being pious and truthful and unselfish.

In those days little boys did not have many books written for them. People did not like their children to read stories; and cheap picture-books had not been invented. But David read his Bible a good deal, and he was very fond of studying the great book of Nature. I mean that he loved to roam along the banks of the Clyde, looking for fossils and flowers and butterflies. From this he learned the habit of observing little things that other people did not notice; and that proved of very great value to him when he grew up and travelled in places where other white people had never been. David's father was very fond of books of travel, and he told his boys about the adventures of explorers and missionaries in far-off lands; while David's mother told her children stories of Scottish history. So, though the lad had not many books, he learned a great deal from his parents.

When he was ten years old, David left school and went to work in a cotton-mill amidst the rattle of machinery. And what do you think he did with the money his mother gave him for himself out of his first week's wages? He bought a book, not a story-book with pictures like boys and girls of ten buy now—but a Latin Grammar! And when he was tending his loom in the cotton-mill, he propped up the book so that he could glance at it for a minute and learn his declensions. Afterwards he bought other books, and read and studied at a night-school. Fancy going to school at eight o'clock at night after working from six o'clock in the morning! Night school finished at ten, then he would go home to supper and read until twelve o'clock or later, until sometimes his mother had to take his books away and send him off to bed. I expect poor David tumbled into bed at nights very, very tired; and when the bell rang for him to get up at five o'clock next morning, he must have wished that there was more than one Sunday in every week.

Now I do not want you to think that David was anything but a thorough boy, with heaps of fun in him, and perhaps a little mischief, too. I am sure he was a regular right-down fun-loving boy, or he

would not have grown into such a cheerful, brave
man. He enjoyed a frolic, and above everything
he liked to get a rod and line, and to go fishing.
Once he caught a salmon, which really he ought
not to have kept; but he did not think God put
fish into rivers for rich people to keep for themselves, so he took it home. And how do you think
he did it? He slipped the salmon down one leg of
his brother's trousers. As the boys walked home
the villagers were very sorry for Charlie, because
they thought his swollen leg must be hurting him
very badly.

David was a religious boy, but he did not say
very much about it. He tried to be good without
talking about his own goodness. His Sunday-
school teacher told him to make religion the
everyday business of his life, not a thing of fits and
starts; adding, that if he did that, temptations
would not get the better of him. The time came
when David made Jesus the King of his life;
but he remembered always that Jesus said that
He would know his disciples by their fruits. So
he set himself to be known as one of Christ's men,
not by what he said, but by what he was. And
that is a very good way, too.

How David Livingstone came to be a missionary is a rather long story. But I must tell you
that it was a letter written by a German missionary in China that first set his heart burning to
go and tell the heathen about Jesus and His love.
This German missionary's name was Gutzlaff,
but you must pronounce it as if it were spelt

Gootslav. Gutzlaff was a very good man; and the letter he wrote to England saying how much the Chinese needed Jesus as their Saviour, made David want to go out to China and work alongside Gutzlaff. But David wanted to be able to cure the sick bodies of the Chinese, as a doctor, as well as to save their souls by preaching the Gospel of Jesus Christ. There were not many medical missionaries at that time, and to be trained as a doctor cost a lot of money. Now David Livingstone, as I have told you, was poor; but he was also very determined. So he worked hard all through the summer months in the cotton-mill, saving every penny he could, so as to go to a medical college at Glasgow all the winter. Even then he could not pay all his college fees, and he had to borrow a little money from his brother, and pay it back later.

Besides being diligent in his studies, David was clever with his hands. He could use all kinds of tools and do all sorts of odd jobs; and many years afterwards he used to say that being a Jack-of-all-trades was a great help to him when he was journeying in Africa far away from blacksmiths and wheelwrights who could mend his wagons. When he had been studying medicine for two years, David went to the London Missionary Society and asked them to send him out to China; but a war was raging in China, and the Society decided to let Livingstone go to Africa.

David's interest in Africa was aroused at a meeting at which Dr. Moffat, another famous missionary, spoke of his work in that great continent. Dr. Moffat was then working at Kuruman in Bechuanaland, and he told David after the meeting that from his headquarters there, he could see the smoke of a thousand villages to which no missionary had ever been to take the Gospel story. But before he could be a missionary at all David had to go to college again—this time at a little town in Essex called Ongar.

I ought to tell you about a long walk David took one day when he was a student at Ongar. He wanted to see a relative of his father's who was in London, twenty-four miles away. There was no train or bus, so David walked all the way. Then when he had seen his relative he set out to walk back to Ongar; but on the way he stopped to help a lady who had fallen out of a carriage and hurt herself. Then he missed the road, and walked a long distance off his track; but at last by starlight, he found a sign-post that put him on the right road again. It was twelve o'clock at night when he reached Ongar, and he had been walking since three in the morning. Of course he was tired out and white with exhaustion, and somebody had to put him to bed. He had walked nearly sixty miles in one day. But, my, wasn't he tired! Do you know, he slept until Sunday after-noon! I expect you would have wanted to sleep until Monday afternoon if you had been as tired as he was.

II

TO AFRICA

By the time David was ready to go out to Africa as a missionary, he had grown into a very strong young man. People noticed two things about him that were what we call characteristic: he had fine eyes like his mother had—coaxing eyes with a kind gleam in them. Yet no one can say whether they were blue or hazel eyes. Perhaps people who looked at him saw so much kindness in his eyes that they forgot to notice what colour they were. And the other thing people noticed about David Livingstone was his walk. It was a slow, steady, swinging gait—as if he could go on walking for ever, and as if fire, water, and stone-walls would never stop him.

If you were going to South Africa to-day it would not be very much of an adventure. A fast train would take you to Southampton, a big steamer would carry you over the sea to Cape Town, and another train would take you right over the veldt to the heart of the Dark Continent, or by plane in a few hours. But when David went out to Africa, in 1840, things were very different. He sailed from London in a ship called the *George*, and on the way to South Africa the ship called at Rio de Janeiro, which is a port in South America.

This made the voyage very roundabout, and it took as many months as you would take weeks or hours to get to Cape Town now.

Not very much was known about Africa when Livingstone went there. The coast-line was inhabited here and there by white people; and a few brave people, mostly missionaries, had pushed their way a bit into the interior. Livingstone went first to a place called Kuruman, where only black-faced people lived. A great missionary named Robert Moffat was at work there, and in his home Livingstone stayed, and met Mary Moffat. He fell in love with Mary, and, later, they were married, and lived happily ever after. But on this first visit David did not stay long at Kuruman, because he was bent on being a pioneer.

Now you know a pioneer is a man who goes where other people have never been. David Livingstone wanted to do that. There were hundreds of thousands of savages who had never heard of Jesus Christ, and he made journeys among them without any fear that they would injure him. When he was on these pioneering trips, David had to live on very funny food. One day he had rhinoceros steak, which he says, was "toughness itself." Wherever he went he did good. He doctored the sore eyes of a chief and made a friend of him. One day a little girl of twelve years of age hid under his wagon. She had run away because she was going to be sold as a slave. A man with a gun came to take her away, but the little girl took off the beads which she wore, and so bribed the man to go away. Then Livingstone hid her away. "Though fifty men had come for her," he said, "they would not have got her." That is the kind of man David Livingstone was—always helping somebody out of trouble.

When David saved that little black girl from being sold as a slave, he did not know that doing it would change the whole course of his life. But it did. It was his first sight of that horrible thing we call slavery. David found that Africa was cursed by this awful trade in men and women and children. The black people lived in tribes, which were always fighting and making prisoners. They took the prisoners and loaded them with heavy wooden chains so that they could not run away, and they sold them to slave-traders. When a man is a slave he belongs to some one else, who can do just what he likes with him, even kill him if he likes. The women were sold too, and even the little children. This wicked trade made David Livingstone furious with anger, and he set himself to stop it. How he helped to do it, you shall hear later.

Some white people look down on black men and women because of the colour of their skin; but Livingstone loved the negroes of Africa, and he really gave his life to them. He knew God made both white and black people, and that God does not care what colour people's skins may be, so long as their hearts are clean and their lives good.

Not all the natives that Livingstone saw were black. Some of them were little brown people called Bushmen. And they were very clever, too.

There were other people with very funny names—
names taken from animals. You know that in
savage countries the people often make a god of an
animal—they call it their Totem. Now in Africa
the natives did this. One tribe had taken a crocodile as their Totem, and called themselves Bakwena (Ba—people; Kwena—crocodile) or People
of the Crocodile. Livingstone spent some time with
the Bakwena, and as he was kind to them—
curing their sicknesses and teaching them useful
things without being afraid of them—they got
fond of him. Then he went among the Bakhatlas
(People of the Monkey), and learned their language, too, so that he could teach them about
Jesus and about the right way to live. He made his
home at a place called Mabotsa, a name meaning
marriage-feast, and there he took Mary Moffat
when she became his wife.

One day a little baby boy came to their home.
David and Mary were very proud of this little
white baby; but the Bakhatla people, who had
never seen anything but black babies, were very
puzzled and amused at it. This little white baby
was christened Robert, and as the Bakhatla call a
mother by her first boy's name, they called Mrs.
Livingstone Ma-Robert—the mother of Robert.

I wonder if any one has ever told you the story
of David Livingstone and the lion. It is almost as
famous as the story of King David and his lion.
One day, when he was at Mabotsa, some natives
came running to Livingstone to say that a lion
had sprung upon their cattle in the daytime and

killed several cows. It was an unheard of thing for a lion, which only prowls by night in search of prey and generally sleeps under a bush all the day, to come out in the sunlight and attack cattle. The Mabotsa people were frightened, and thought they were bewitched. These poor people believed in witches and went in living dread of evil spirits. And when the lion came again and killed nine sheep in the daytime, Livingstone thought it was time to do something. He took his gun and gave another gun to one of the natives whom he had trained as a teacher, and they set out for the crest of a hill topped with low trees, where the lions were believed to be hiding. Soon they came within sight of a lion. It was sitting on a rock, and the native teacher fired. His bullet missed its mark but hit the rock under the lion, which bit at the spot where the lead bullet had spluttered. Then it jumped down and dashed through the ring of natives. Two more lions got away without being shot, and the Bakhatlas were now very alarmed, because the lions would be mad after that. They got the wind up, as the soldiers say when they are frightened.

But Livingstone went on looking for lions, and turning round the end of the hill he saw a great big lion sitting on a piece of rock with a bush in front of it. David took steady aim with his gun and fired twice. He hit it with both bullets, but the lion was not killed. It lashed its tail in anger, and Livingstone put another bullet down the gun-barrel and was ramming the charge home when he heard a shout. He looked half round and saw the lion leaping upon him. The big brute caught his shoulder, and David and the lion went rolling down on the ground together. Then the lion, growling horribly, drove its teeth into the top of Livingstone's left arm, and shook him like a terrier does a rat. Livingstone says he felt no pain and had no feeling of terror, but as he glanced around he saw the native teacher ten yards away, trying to shoot the lion. Both barrels missed fire, but the lion left Livingstone and leapt upon the teacher. Then it jumped on another native who was trying to spear the fierce creature. But before it could do any more harm the lion fell dead from the wounds Livingstone had given it when he first fired. David's left arm was crushed into splinters, and there were eleven tooth-marks that he carried to the end of his life. His left arm was always weak after this encounter with the King of the Beasts, and it hurt him to lift his gun to his shoulder.

Even a noble man like Livingstone found out that there were people who hated him and would do all they could, in a sneaky sort of way, to upset his plans. Sometimes it seems as if the more good a man tries to do, the more enemies he makes but that only makes good men more determined on their good work. David Livingstone was bent on stopping slavery wherever he found it. But near Mabotsa there were some Boers who had come up from Cape Colony. They were not kind to the natives. Indeed, they were very harsh to them, and made them work as slaves. Moreover, they made raids on the native tribes and stole their cattle. The chief 'Sechele, who was Livingstone's friend, lived in dread of these Boers, who encouraged other tribes to attack him and his people. They were always afraid of being attacked unexpectedly and robbed and made slaves. Livingstone did not think badly of all Boers—indeed, he praised them generally as sober and industrious people; but he did not hide his dislike of those Boers who robbed the natives and took part in the slave trade. So they revenged themselves by attacking Livingstone's house and destroying its contents.

All through his life Livingstone never lost a chance of learning about things. When he was on his five months' journey from England to Africa he learned from the captain how to use the ship's sextant and how to tell in what latitude and longitude the ship was. This was done by observations of the sun and the stars. When he got to the Cape and was kept there, he used to go to the Observatory, where Sir Thomas Maclean helped him to study astronomy. This knowledge was of great value to Livingstone when he was making journeys in strange parts of Africa. He had a watch, but he could not have told if it were keeping exact time unless he had been able to check it by the sun; and though his magnetic compass told him where the north was, he wanted to know also in what latitude and longitude he was. So he made what are called astronomical observations, and he made them so carefully and wrote them so exactly in his journals, that a great geographer, named Sir Harry Johnston, has said that Livingstone's actual routes in South Central Africa can be exactly traced now from his writings. In all his descriptions of the things he saw, Livingstone was always very exact, and when you have read his word-picture of an African scene, you can almost imagine that it is there in front of you.

Lots of other adventures came David's way. When he removed from Mabotsa to another village named Chonuane he was driven out by a long drought. No rain fell, and the sun was so hot that all the water dried up. So Livingstone had to remove to another place, near a river called Kolobeng. That was the last house he lived in. Afterwards Livingstone had no home. Lions did not worry them there; but there were wild beasts all around the village. From his own door-step Livingstone shot a rhinoceros and a buffalo; and one evening a man came to Livingstone to say that a fierce black rhinoceros had attacked a hunter's wagon and nearly killed the driver. Though he had to walk ten miles through a forest full of prowling beasts of prey, Livingstone started off at once to try to heal the man. But when he reached the spot the poor man was dead, so David's journey was wasted. He used to say that "the great God had an only Son and he was sent to earth as a Missionary-Physician," and he wanted to follow in the wake of Jesus, and go about doing good. He was never afraid of anything, because Jesus had promised to be "with you to the end," and he said Jesus was a Gentleman of the highest honour, who would keep his word!

Everywhere he went Livingstone kept his eyes wide open. Nothing escaped his notice. He learned this habit when he went on walks along the Clyde as a boy in Scotland; and in South Africa he found thousands of things to interest him. The humming birds, ostriches, antelopes, fossils, flowers, herbs, trees—all these he studied and collected specimens to send to friends in England. Then he learned to do any number of things for himself. He built houses, made gardens, cobbled boots, doctored sick people, tinkered pots and pans, did carpentry, mended guns, farriered horses, repaired wagons, preached, taught, and lectured. He was his own doctor when he fell ill, as he often did, with fever. Isn't it funny to think of David doctoring himself, ordering himself to go to bed, examining his own tongue, and making himself say "ninety-nine" to himself? He mixed his own medicine, so I do not think he had any nasty cough mixture to take. But he must often have been very lonely when he went off on his journeys, leaving Mrs. Livingstone and his children behind him. One little baby died, and then he sent his family to England, because Africa was not healthy for them. To his little girl Agnes, he wrote a lovely letter, saying good-bye. This is what he said:—

"I shall not see you again for a long time, and I am very sorry. I have no nanny now. I have

given you back to Jesus, your friend, your Papa
who is in heaven. He is above you, but he is
always near you when we ask things from Him—
that is, praying to Him; and if you do or say a
naughty thing, ask Him to pardon you, and
bless you, and make you one of his children.
Love Jesus much, for He loves you, and He came
and died for you."

I expect little Agnes was very proud of that
letter. She always kept it, and she let lots of other
boys and girls read it.

III

EXPLORING

NEARBY Livingstone's home there was a desert called the Kalahari. It stretched so far to the north that people thought that all the inside of Africa was a desert. David wanted to find out if this was true. He made up his mind to cross the desert. The chief 'Sechele told him no white man could ever cross it; but David said he would try. He started in a wagon drawn by oxen and soon they were in the midst of the desert of white sand, so soft that the wheels of the wagon sank in it. They saw plenty of wild beasts—antelopes and jackals and hyenas and lions; but there was no water, no wells or rivers—nothing but a sea of soft white sand. But deep down below the sand there was water, and the clever little Bushwomen dug deep holes, put grass at the bottom, and stuck a hollow stick in the hole. Then they filled it up with sand and sucked the water up the stick. They stored the water in ostrich-egg shells, which are as big as a boy's head, and buried the shells in the sand so as to keep the water cool.

This journey across the desert was an awful trial, and David must have wondered if he would get back alive. He saw a very strange thing one day. In the distance he saw a lake, with little waves rippling in the sunlight, and with trees casting soft shadows. They hurried to the water, but as they drew nearer it seemed to go farther away. Really there was no lake. It is what is called a desert mirage, and is made by the sun's rays dancing on the white sand. There was a lake three hundred miles to the north, but it was many days before Livingstone found it. He first discovered a great river and then this great lake, 'Ngami. Though it was a very beautiful spot Livingstone could not stay there long because of a stinging fly called the tsetse, which was very dangerous. When any one has been stung by a tsetse he feels very drowsy, falls asleep, and after a time dies of a fever called sleeping-sickness.

It was a great change for Livingstone to paddle in a native canoe down the river he had found, after all the hardships of travelling in a wagon. He had tried riding on an ox, but its skin was loose, and he slipped about on it just as if he were on a saddle that was not buckled on firmly. And the ox had long horns which it dug into David when it tried to spear a fly that was biting it.

Now when he had found the lake and the river, David Livingstone wanted to discover other things. He was an explorer as well as a missionary. Indeed, he thought it was not much use trying to teach the Central Africans about Jesus until he had found an easier way to reach them than by the long journey from the Cape. He wanted to find a way into the heart of Africa either from the west or the east coast, instead of from the south. And he thought that if he opened a path into the heart of this unknown country he might stop the slave trade, which he called the open sore of the world.

It was to open such a path that David began his expedition from Cape Town to Loanda on the West Coast and later that great journey right across Africa to the East Coast. When all his preparations were complete David set off for the West Coast travelling by ox-wagon—not a very comfortable means of transport as we have already heard, so that we can be sure that when at the end of three months Kuruman came in sight and the first stage of his journey was completed safely, David was very relieved. From Kuruman he went on into the country of the Makololo whose young chief Sekeletu gave Livingstone a great welcome.

For six months David made Linyanti (the capital of the Makololo) his headquarters before proceeding with his journey. There he would gather the natives around him while he told them the stories of Jesus. They listened eagerly for they soon came to know that he not only talked about Jesus and how he went about teaching the people and healing the sick, but was in these ways so like his master that, through the way he lived, many of them came to love Jesus too.

David was counting on Sekeletu to help him plan the long journey to Loanda, and when the time came for a start to be made the chief called an assembly of his people over which he presided. Of course there were some who prophesied that the expedition would fail and tried to discourage the rest from having anything to do with it. But Sekeletu was keenly interested in David's plan because he knew that if he succeeded there was a good chance of trade and prosperity coming to his people. When the assembly ended twenty-seven of the strongest men of the Makololo were chosen to go with David to the West Coast, not as paid servants, but as companions who were as interested in the success of the expedition as David himself.

There were times on this journey when they had run through all the food that they had brought with them. They suffered greatly from hunger and were glad even to be able to make an occasional meal of the mice and moles which they caught on their way. Once as they were crossing a river which was in flood David narrowly escaped being drowned. Whenever they came to a river the oxen were loaded with the baggage and were sent into the water to swim across while the men crossed by clinging on to the tails of the oxen. On this occasion however, before David had got hold of this unusual form of tow rope his ox hurried after his companions leaving David in the middle of the flooded river. So greatly was David loved by his natives that immediately they saw what had happened about twenty of them dived into the water to rescue him, but David had always been a powerful swimmer and he managed, despite the fast flowing currents, to reach the opposite bank safely. The natives, who did not know until then that he could swim almost as well as themselves, were delighted at this demonstration that he could "carry himself across a river."

Passing through the country of the Chiboques one day their encampment was completely surrounded by Njambe the chief and a dangerous looking band of warriors who waved their swords in the air and seemed to be planning an immediate attack. David's natives grasped their spears prepared to stand their ground when the attack came, but David, anxious as always to avoid any bloodshed, calmly unfolded his camp stool and sat down. Then he asked the chief to come forward and sit opposite him that they might have a parley. Njambe with some of his counsellors came forward, but his warriors also closed in and threatened David and his natives with their swords and guns. It must have taken a lot of courage to sit and talk calmly with all those guns pointed at him; David realised he was in very great danger but he knew that God was with him and that made all the difference. Quietly he told Njambe that all he wanted was to be allowed to pass through his country in peace. At first Njambe refused this request altogether, but David told him that he would not strike first and that if there was a battle the responsibility for it would rest with Njambe. At last when the chief had received presents of beads and clothing the parley ended happily and David was allowed to carry on his journey without a single shot having been fired.

Many were the hardships suffered by David and his men, arising chiefly from the lack of proper food and the nature of the country through which they were passing. There were times when David was so sick with fever that he could not go on, but had to wait until the fever had left him.

The best of men will sometimes lose heart. David never did that because he believed all the time that God had sent him to Africa to open up that great continent and until his work was done he believed that he would be given strength to carry on. Some of the Makololo who were with him began to doubt whether they would ever reach the sea coast, and once they had begun to be afraid that their journey was in vain they began to grumble, and, as David took no notice of their complaints, they staged an open mutiny and declared their intention of returning home to Linyanti. David had already had ample proof of their courage, and he knew that it was not fear of hardship which had caused this trouble so he did not reproach them but tried with kind words to show them that the end of their journey was now in sight, and that if they would have faith a little longer they would shortly be able to laugh at the idea that they had thought of going home when success was so near at hand. To this they listened in silence so David quietly told them that he himself intended to go on even if he had to travel alone, then entering his tent he knelt down and prayed to God to help him to be brave that he might finish the work that God had given him to do.

David's determination to go on alone had made a great impression upon the Makololo and very soon they felt ashamed that they had proved unfaithful. When David rose from his knees he found the "mutineers" waiting to speak with him. They asked for forgiveness and promised that they would never leave him but would follow him faithfully to the end of the journey. How glad David must have been to hear these words and how proud of the loyal way in which they kept this promise.

At last they reached Cassange where they were all made very welcome by some friendly Portuguese who lived there, and after a well-earned rest they said good-bye and set off on the last few hundred miles to the sea. The Makololo, who had never before seen the sea, were so amazed when they eventually reached the coast that they asked David if they had come to the end of the world.

The long journey together with the many attacks of fever which Livingstone had suffered made it essential for him to take a long rest in Loanda. Mr. Gabriel, a Commissioner appointed by the British Government for putting an end to the slave trade, took David into his home and promptly put him to bed. How glad he was to be in a comfortable bed again after nearly a year sleeping on the ground.

It was four months before David was well
enough to set out again. During that time his
Makololo natives waited for him to get better
without complaining and set to work to earn
their living. They hit on the idea of collecting
firewood and selling it in bundles to the people
of Loanda. It was hard work as they had to go
long distances to collect wood and then carry it
to Loanda on their backs.

There were three British cruisers at Loanda
patrolling the seas to keep a watch on any ships
that might be trying to run a cargo of slaves.
One day a coal ship arrived to bring supplies to
the cruisers, and Mr. Gabriel arranged that
David's Makololo natives should be given a chance
to earn some money by unloading the coal ship
on to the cruisers. How excited they were on
seeing the cruisers at close quarters, they were
like huge villages all made of iron; and floating
on the water!

I wonder what you would have done in David's
place if you had been offered a passage home to
England from Loanda? That is what did happen,
and the thought of sailing home at that moment
in one of the cruisers must have seemed very
inviting. No more hunger, no more sleeping on
the hard ground and above all no more fever!
But David chose to stay at Loanda determined
that as soon as he was better he would return to
Linyanti with the Makololo natives whom
Sekeletu had allowed to come with him. They
were prepared to do any kind of work while they

waited for their "father" as they fondly called
David, and if he went back to England now,
although his health was bad, he felt that he would
be deserting them. Besides he was eager to reach
Linyanti again to prepare for the next great
journey he was already planning—to find a path
to the east coast. We realise just how brave David
was in deciding to stay in Africa when we know
that the journey back took him a whole year.

Great was the excitement of the Makololo
when, after nearly two years away from home,
they came in sight of Linyanti. Dressing themselves in the fine materials which they had bought
in Loanda with the money that they had earned,
they fell into line as they had seen the soldiers do
in their drill at Loanda with their guns over their
shoulders; what a welcome they received as they
marched along and how glad Sekeletu was to
see David again. While they were all excited
about their safe return, David called them to a
service to give thanks to God who had looked
after them and brought them back safely through
so many dangers on the journey.

David spent seven weeks in Linyanti making
plans for a new expedition to the East Coast and
once again he was counting on Sekeletu to provide
him with men to go with him. This time when
Sekeletu called an assembly of his people together
and explained David's plans, hardly had he
finished speaking before more than a hundred
had volunteered to go with him. The twenty-
seven who had made the journey to Loanda were

so full of praise for their "father" and had told
so many stories of their adventures that even
David was surprised at the number who volunteered.

Sekeletu and two hundred of his followers
decided to accompany David as far as Kalai.
The whole company were fed at the chief's
expense from cattle which he commanded his
followers to take with them. Among the baggage
were all sorts of things which Sekeletu had provided for the use of David and his men during
the journey, including beads and cloth which
could be used to buy the favour of war-like
tribes or to purchase a canoe or supplies of meal.
Nor did David forget to include a supply of flour
so that he could bake his own bread—something
he had very much missed on his last journey—
in a home-made oven.

On the second night, when some of the men
had gone on ahead with the supplies, which
included a change of clothes for David, there was
a terrific thunderstorm which not only drenched
the party but completely soaked the ground on
which they intended to pass the night. David did
not look forward to that prospect one little bit,
and he was greatly moved by the kindness of
Sekeletu who offered him his own dry blanket,
telling David that he was used to sleeping rough
whether it was wet or fine and, without waiting
to see what David would say about his generous
offer, he lay down and rested on the cold wet
ground until morning.

Some day you must read Livingstone's own story of his great journey across Africa from the West coast to the East coast. Only a very brave man would have attempted it; only a very strong man, moved by a holy purpose, could have done it. No one had ever done it before. There was no road, not even a track. The people he passed through were cruel savages, dirty, ugly, and cowardly. The heat was terrible, and fever made David very weak sometimes. He could not preach to the people, but he had a little magic lantern, and he showed them slides of Bible stories. Although they liked the pictures, the poor, ignorant savages, full of fears, were afraid lest the figures in the pictures should enter their bodies as evil spirits. On one occasion some savages would have stopped Livingstone from crossing a river, but he took out his watch and let them listen to its ticking. Then he let the sun's rays pass through a small magnifying glass that he had in his pocket, and it acted as a burning glass and caused fire to burn. The natives were so amazed at these wonders that they let David cross in their canoe to the other side of the river.

IV

ACROSS AFRICA

LIVINGSTONE'S discovery of a way to the East coast was one of the greatest feats. During his journey to the West coast he had won the hearts of the Makololo natives, who had travelled with him. You may imagine how careful he was of their well-being, from the fact that he brought back to their native village, every man who had set out on the journey with him. Not a single life was lost, though they had gone through grave perils from man and beast. Livingstone kept his word to a savage black man just as he did to a white man; so he proved to the people of Africa what an English Christian is. He said that much of his influence depended on the good name given him by the Bakwena (the tribe he first worked among), and he secured that only through a long course of tolerably good conduct. "No one," he said, "ever gains much influence in this country without purity and uprightness." Livingstone could not afford to pay his black people much for their services, and it must have been the love he inspired that made them so loyal and true.

When Sekeletu said good-bye to David at Kalai the expedition now consisted of 115 people, David and 114 of the Makololo many

of whom were to carry the baggage all the way
to the coast.

We sometimes see a traveller in England with
two or three porters looking after his luggage,
and we wonder why he wants to have so many
trunks and boxes; but here was Livingstone with
114 men. But we have to remember that Livingstone was journeying on foot, and not by train.
Everything he needed had to be carried on men's
heads in small packages, because the journey
took them through closely-grown forests, across
rivers, and over hills, so each man could carry
only a little weight, especially as the sun poured
its heat fiercely upon them. Many of the men
would be needed to carry the food for the big
party, and the blankets and cooking utensils. I
don't think they carried any tents, as Livingstone
seems to have slept on the ground sometimes in
his clothes, though he generally liked to change
into other clothes to sleep. And though it was
very hot by day it was often very cold at night.
Livingstone and his bearers travelled in a long
single file like Indians do.

At night he used to write up his journals and
make notes of what he had seen. Over these he
took great care. Once on his western journey
Livingstone had sent home his journal of observations, along with some maps he had drawn, but
the steamer was wrecked on its voyage to England.
It took Livingstone some months to write his
journal again and re-draw the maps; but he did
it without groaning. We may safely assume that

Livingstone took great care of the notes and
observations he made. Over one of his discoveries
he had a disappointment. He had come to the
conclusion that the centre of Africa (which
people had thought was a desert) was like a
great saucer with hills all round it making the
rim. And he satisfied himself that there had once
been a great lake there. Also he was convinced
that this country would be fertile, and would
grow coffee and cotton and vegetable-oil pods.
Another traveller, Sir Roderick Murchison, had,
however, come to the same conclusion before
Livingstone, and without Livingstone knowing
of it. So the credit of a very important geographical discovery went to some one else.

If Livingstone did not get credit for finding
out what the contour of Africa was like, he had
the joy of making another very great discovery.
While he was on this journey to the East coast,
he heard from some of the natives about a "smoke
that sounds." This was the poor, ignorant black
man's way of describing the mist thrown up by
a great waterfall. Livingstone at last came to
the spot, and his were the first eyes of a white
man to gaze on the marvels of the Zambezi
River Falls. Livingstone, who had seen so many
great sights, said it was the most wonderful sight
he had witnessed in Africa. A mighty river over
a mile wide rushes along till it reaches a chasm,
over which it falls nearly 400 feet. Below the fall
the river channel is narrow, and the wide stream
is squeezed into about a hundred yards. Columns

of fine misty spray, two or three thousand feet high, leap into the air, and are blown about by the breeze. From an islet at the top of the falls Livingstone watched this majestic spectacle. Then he planted coffee beans as well as apricot and peach stones by the edge of the falls, hoping that trees would grow. Livingstone gave the falls the name "Victoria Falls," in honour of Queen Victoria, and he carved "D.L., 1855"—his own initials and the year of his discovery—on a tree growing near by. Then he thought that he had been guilty of a piece of vanity; but he excused it, as it was the only instance when he had been vain. Still, a man who first discovered such a wonderful sight as the Victoria Falls had some right to be just a little tiny bit vain. Don't you think so?

A very pretty compliment was paid to Livingstone while he was making this great Eastern journey. Generally when he was going through a strange land he asked leave from the tribe who owned it to pass through their country, explaining that he was on a peaceful errand. Once or twice suspicious tribes—and we must not blame them for being suspicious, because they often had very good reason to be afraid of visitors—would bar the way. On one occasion when he asked for leave to pass, a black man rushed out with an axe to stop Livingstone, who thought he was going to have his head chopped off by a mad savage, and felt that would be a sorry way to leave the world. But on this occasion a

pretty compliment was paid to Livingstone. He
was prevented by a howling mob of natives from
crossing the Zambezi River. Then some one asked
him who he was, and Livingstone answered, "I
am an Englishman!" "Ah," said the natives, who
lived near a Portuguese Settlement, "you must
be one of that tribe that loves the black man,"
and then Livingstone was allowed to pass. Soon
after that the journey was ended at a place called
Quilimane, where he saw the sea, and knew that
he had opened a new way into Central Africa.

After crossing Africa, which was a great feat,
Livingstone, who had been fifteen years without
a holiday, came home to England. He was grieved
to find his father dead; but he was glad to see his
wife and his children again. I expect they had some
fine yarns told them about his adventures, and
were very proud of their brave, good father! All
England was proud of him, too. Queen Victoria
sent for him to hear his story from his own lips,
and all kinds of great people went to listen to
his lectures. He was given a gold medal by the
Royal Geographical Society, and the book that
he wrote was read by every one who could buy,
or borrow a copy. The Directors of the London
Missionary Society made a hero of David, and
when he asked for more missionaries to go out to
the heart of Africa, they promised to send them.

Soon Livingstone, though he loved being in
England, yearned to be back in Africa. The Dark
Continent called him, and the welfare of the
African people was on his heart. He wanted to

go back to make an open path for Christianity and commerce.

This time David did not go out from the London Missionary Society but as a servant of the British Government. Now I don't want you to think that David was no longer a Christian missionary. He remained a missionary to the end of his life. David was what we sometimes call a pioneer which means that he went on ahead of others opening up new roads and exploring lands and discovering peoples never before visited by the white man. Thus it was as a pioneer and as an explorer that David returned, for much as he would have loved to continue working under the London Missionary Society they had not enough money to arrange this journey, and David was certain that this and other such journeys must be made if the way was to be opened up for the Gospel to reach the people in the heart of Africa.

Lord Palmerston, who was then Prime Minister, and Lord Clarendon, the head of the Foreign Office, provided David with money and equipment for a journey into the valley of the River Zambezi. This was the first journey where other white men went with him including Dr. Kirk who wanted to study the plant life of Africa. His brother Charles Livingstone accompanied David to act as his secretary and help him write up his reports on all that they saw on their journey. Captain Bedingfield came as skipper of the small steamer which was to be taken out in pieces and fitted together before being launched on the River Shire. This steamer specially made, as was hoped, for the navigation of the River Zambezi was named the *Ma-Robert*, which you will remember was Mrs. Livingstone's African name.

Alas, the *Ma-Robert* was a great disappointment to David, everything that could go wrong with a ship seemed to go wrong with it. First its boiler-fire ate up too much fuel, then its engines were noisy and did not work smoothly. The steamer wheezed like you do when you have a bad cold on your chest. So Livingstone called it "The Asthmatic."

V

BY RIVER AND LAKE

WHEN the party reached the mouth of the Zambezi the *Ma-Robert* was fixed together and in it they set sail to examine the various inlets of the river. Now the Portuguese had always said that only one of these inlets could be used for ships and all the maps that were printed only marked the Kilimane as navigable, but David soon discovered that the maps were wrong.

There were four inlets to the river apart from the Kilimane and they were all of them suitable for shipping. David realised that the Portuguese had printed these maps all wrong for a wicked purpose of their own. They wanted to keep the British cruisers watching the Kilimane while they used the other routes for collecting cargoes of slaves without interference. What a good thing that David discovered their wicked plan and was able, by having true maps sent home to the British Government, to strike one more blow in the fight to stop slavery.

Steaming up the Kangare, one of the tributaries of the Zambezi, they made slow progress as far as Tete where David had left his Makololo to wait for his return from England. Great was their joy when they recognised him, though at first they were afraid to touch him lest they should spoil his new clothes. What a lot they had to tell him of their adventures while he had been away. They had been treated very kindly by Major Sicard of the Portuguese garrison who had given them land to grow their own food, but they had faced real hardships too. Six had been killed by Bonga a hostile native chief and thirty had died of smallpox.

It was impossible owing to the rapids which extended for more than eight miles along the river to make progress in the *Ma-Robert* so from Tete a report to the British Government was sent asking for a more suitable ship to be sent out. Meantime, leaving the *Ma-Robert* at Tete, the party set off overland in the direction of an inland lake which they decided to explore. This turned out to be Lake Shirwa—a great sheet of water surrounded by swamp.

At one native village ruled by a chief called Tingane, about 500 armed men blocked the path of Livingstone and his party. It looked a very dangerous situation ; but Livingstone boldly went forward and asked to meet the headmen of the tribe. He explained that they had come in peace and only wanted to explore the lands beyond. Tingane at first was afraid that David and his party had come hunting for slaves and that explained this show of force. When he knew why David had come and heard how he was set against the slave trade he was most friendly and called his people together. The chief explained to his people that they had nothing to fear from these men who only wanted to help the people of Africa. Well might Tingane and his people oppose the progress of the white man for until David and his party reached Lake Shirwa, the only white men they had seen had had no love for the Africans and had only come in search of slaves to sell in Europe. Many were the brave battles that Tingane and his people had fought to keep their liberty.

They embarked once more in the *Ma-Robert* and slowly progressed about 200 miles until they reached a number of cataracts which they named "The Murchison" after Sir Roderick Murchison who had proved a great friend to the expedition. The crocodiles surprised by this invasion of their kingdom several times rushed towards the ship as if they intended an attack, but having at close quarters gained some idea of its size they must have thought better of it and retreated.

Supplies being now exhausted, they made their way down river again to the Kangare where they were able to obtain fresh provisions from one of the British cruisers which was on duty there. The *Ma-Robert* had to be beached this time for repairs, but when the job was completed they set off again towing behind several smaller boats in which supplies and men for which there was no room in the *Ma-Robert* were carried. Unfortunately one of the Makololo was drowned when one of these boats capsized.

At a place called Mboma they laid in fresh supplies of food and as they were staying the night there, one of the natives who reckoned he was a musician, decided to entertain them by playing on an instrument with one string, the like of which David had never seen before. After a while the entertainment, which was specially for David's benefit—the musician never having seen a white man before—became rather monotonous and David was glad to put an end to the concert by making a present of a piece of cloth to the musician—the equivalent in Africa of "giving him a penny to go into the next street."

Leaving the *Ma-Robert* in the care of the rest of the party, David set off with three of his English companions and 36 Makololo to search for Lake Nyassa. Many were the strange people they met on the way; they were generally friendly when David had explained his object at a palaver, and often willing to help him with such supplies as he required for the journey.

Of all the strange ornaments which the natives are accustomed to wear the strangest that David saw were the Pelele worn by Mansanja women. The upper lip is pierced and the hole is gradually widened until there is a gap of about two inches, into this an ivory ring is forced until the lip stretches a couple of inches beyond the end of the nose.

Livingstone and Dr. Kirk were the first Europeans to see Lake Nyassa, one of the three largest

African lakes. When they eventually reached the southernmost point there lay before them a lake so tremendous in extent that they had no means of knowing its length. Later they were to discover that it stretched for over 300 miles, about as far as from London to Edinburgh.

David now felt it was time to return to Linyanti to take back the Makololo who had been in his service for so long. Not all of them went with him for some had married in Tete and preferred to settle there, and others had unfortunately taken to the evil ways of some of the half-cast people of Tete who were heavy drinkers. Leaving the *Ma-Robert* in the care of ten English sailors in Tete, David set out with Dr. Kirk, his brother and the remainder of the Makololo.

Progress was slow, partly due to the terrific heat of the sun, which made the earth and the rocks almost unbearable to the bare feet of the natives. David managed to keep them on the march for about six hours each day, walking about two miles an hour, but even then the natives complained of being tired. Living in Tete had spoiled them for the more energetic kind of life that they had always been used to when Livingstone first travelled with them from Linyanti.

As they passed through the Chicova plains a chief named Chitora came out to meet the party to welcome them and make them a present

of food and drink. He told them he had heard
of Dr. Livingstone and had always wanted to
meet him as he knew that he was a friend to the
people of Africa. Anything he had was there
for David and his party to use. It must have
warmed David's heart to know that he was not
only opening up new ways into the heart of Africa
but was finding a way into the heart of her
peoples too.

The journey took them among many strange
tribes. The Batokas for example had never seen
any white men before and were at first very
alarmed by their appearance. They told David
that their fathers had never told them about
people like him. They said that they had seen
stranger things therefore, than any of their
ancestors in seeing him and his two companions.
A doubtful compliment but no doubt Livingstone
appreciated their friendly interest.

As they approached Linyanti they were sad
to hear that a mission which had followed David
there several years before had failed. It was not
a healthy neighbourhood for Europeans and of
the nine who had settled there five had died
within a year. The rest, some of whom were sick
with fever, had moved to another place.

At Linyanti they received a welcome, but it
was nothing like the welcome they had on their
return from Loanda. The reason was soon plain.
Sekeletu had contracted leprosy and in his illness
had forgotten much of David's teaching about
the Love of God. He now believed that he had

been bewitched and that his leprosy was some kind of a curse. David was sad to find his old friend so ill and at once went to call on him where he lay away from his own people in a covered wagon. He was glad to see David again. A woman witch doctor was attending him when David arrived; he ordered her to leave him that he might try the white man's medicine. David did everything he could for him and not only tried to cure him of his leprosy but also tried to give him back his faith in the Good News of the Loving Father who sent his son into the world to save the African and the Englishman and who made no difference between them.

It is a pity to think that this great people—the Makololo—were shortly to lose their power and influence as a tribe, but with their chief a sick man that is what happened. A few years after Sekeletu died the great kingdom which he had ruled so wisely since the age of 18 was broken up.

At Linyanti David discovered that all his medical supplies had been kept safely by the trustworthy people of Sekeletu. The missionaries who had been working there during David's absence had all the medicines they needed to cure their diseases, of which some of them had died, within a few yards of their camp, though it is unlikely that they knew that such help was so near at hand.

Although they would not have thought of touching David's property while he was away and although they accepted the teaching of the Bible, David found that they were not so careful about stealing cattle from their neighbours. When he told them that this was wrong they could not understand why. Had their neighbours any right to cattle if they could not fight for them? Besides these cattle that they had taken were probably directly descended from the cattle which at one time had belonged to the father of Sekeletu, so could it be stealing to take back what had once been theirs. David often had experience of their lack of responsibility with the property of others. On one occasion the natives were grumbling that the journey was too long, and David saw that they were getting rebellious and were likely to start stealing his stuff to prevent him from going on. In order to stop them Livingstone dashed out of his shelter waving his pistol and looking as if he meant business. The natives soon listened to him as he warned them that they were not to think that they could take things which did not belong to them. As they became more reasonable we can hear his voice growing less severe, and then he forgave them for their bad conduct. It was always his way to forgive others for their mistakes, he said that he did this because he always found that he often made mistakes himself.

This time when David and his small party set out to return to Kongone, Sekeletu was too ill to go with him but not so ill as to forget to supply food and oxen for the journey, besides a number of canoes for travelling down the valley of the Zambezi.

It was as they crossed the Mburuma rapids that once again David had cause to be grateful to his Makololo followers. As they were crossing the rapids two of the canoes filled with water. Jumping out of the canoes they swam alongside until they reached the foot of the rapid and then ran alongshore to begin baling the water out. Had they not done so it is more than likely that everyone in them would have been drowned. It was in moments like this that they proved how much they loved David—even more than their own lives.

At Tete where you will remember they had left the *Ma-Robert* they bought what supplies they could and set off for Kongone. The *Ma-Robert* now not only wheezed and coughed but refused to keep afloat at all and had to be abandoned. When they reached Kongone the party were welcomed at a new Portuguese customs house where they settled while they awaited the arrival of a ship. Their new ship the *Pioneer* came just before two cruisers which brought with them Bishop Mackenzie and the Oxford and Cambridge missions to the Shire and Lake Nyassa which consisted of six Englishmen and five coloured men from the Cape. They were hoping that David would be able to take them to the Shire but as he was planning an expedition to Rovuma they decided to go with him to see if they could reach lake Nyassa and the Shire that way, but they ran into shallow water and decided to return to the sea. From there they sailed for the mouth of the Zambezi and progressed up the river as far as the Shire up which they sailed as far as Chibisa's village.

VI

FREEING SLAVES

AT Chibisa's they heard that war had broken out in the Manganja country and that a party of slaves would shortly pass through the village on the way to Tete. David who hated the very idea of slavery consulted his friends, and Bishop Mackenzie and his party, and they decided to do all that they could to free the slaves.

Soon a long line of men, women and children, eighty-four in all, appeared manacled together. Sadly they marched, driven along by black drivers armed with muskets. When they caught sight of David and his party the drivers with one exception fled into the forest. The one who remained said that he had bought the slaves and that they were his property, but the slaves said that they had been captured in war. Seeing that David was more ready to believe the slaves than himself he too ran off after the other drivers into the forest.

The captives knelt down and expressed their thanks for this unexpected delivery. They had feared that they were doomed to spend the rest of their lives in slavery. You can imagine that it was not long before David and his followers had cut the ropes which bound the women and

children, but it was more difficult to release the
men as each man had his neck in a forked stick
six or seven feet long and kept in place by an iron
rod which was riveted at both sides across his
throat. Fortunately the Bishop had a hacksaw
in his luggage and one by one the men were freed.
David took up the wooden yokes and broke them
in pieces on the ground.

When they were freed David told them to
prepare a meal and cook it for themselves and for
their children. They could hardly believe their
good fortune but when they saw the kind faces of
these strangers who began to help them light a
fire to boil their pots they soon set to with a will.
A short while before they had been bowed down
by sadness, now they began to laugh and smile
again as the broken yokes were used to make the
fire blaze up.

Many of these people were little children of
four and under. One little boy said to David,
"The others tied us up and starved us; you cut
the ropes and tell us to eat. What sort of people
are you?" How surprised he and the other ex-
slaves would have been if they had known that
these men who had set them free had a Master,
too, who said, "Take my yoke upon you,"
especially if they had understood that His yoke
would bring them not pain, sadness and despair
but love, joy and peace.

When David told the freed slaves that they
might go where they pleased or remain with the
party all they chose to stay with their new friends,

and in the next few days they were to see many
more slaves freed as they had been. One of them
named Chuma became so fond of David that he
became inseparable from him and went with
him on all his journeys. He remained faithful to
David to the end of his life and did a very brave
thing—about which I will tell you soon—after
Livingstone's death. All through his life in Africa
David was trying to stop the slave trade and
while others had awakened the minds and con-
sciences of people at home to this great evil he
did more perhaps than any man to end this
dreadful traffic which was still being carried on
despite the fact that it was against the law.

The bishop and his missionaries settled in
among the Manganja people at Magomero. It was
a hard time for them to begin their work for while
the Manganja were friendly, they were at war
with the Ajawa who were responsible for making
slaves of all those whom they captured in battle.
It was natural that Bishop Mackenzie and his
workers who hated slavery as much as David did,
should have wanted to follow the Ajawa, drive
them out of the Manganja country and free any
slaves they found on the way. David knowing
these tribes a lot better advised them not to do so,
not because he was afraid of the Ajawa, but
because he knew that if he became involved in a
tribal war there would be real danger to the
mission and all its workers.

When David left the mission settlement which
they built at Magomero to set off for lake Nyassa

they were full of hope about the future of their
work among the Manganja. All went well for a
time until one day two of the missionaries together
with a number of Manganja natives set out to
find a quicker route to the Shire. Unfortunately
they lost their way and found themselves in a slave
trading village. Knowing that their lives were in
danger they prepared to go back the way they had
come but the hostile inhabitants seized two of
the Manganjas and the rest barely escaped with
their lives.

Back at Magomero they told their experiences,
and the wives of the two Manganja men who
had been taken as slaves persuaded Bishop
Mackenzie that he ought to go to their rescue.
It was difficult to decide what it was best to do,
but in the end he decided to attack the village.
While David would have been in favour of
seeking a peaceful means to free the men who had
become slaves, he was saddened later when he
heard that the village had also been burned
as a punishment, feeling certain that his Master
would not have approved, and knowing too, that
such an action was going to make it harder for
the missionary in Africa whose job it was to
preach the Gospel of Love. The end of this mission
came soon afterwards. Bishop Mackenzie and
several of his companions died, stricken with
fever. Bishop Tozer, who followed on to take
Mackenzie's place, decided to move the mission
from Magomero to Zanzibar, an island base away
from the unrest between the tribes, but alas also

away from the Manganja people, who badly
needed help at this time when their country was
being overrun by slave traders.

While he was resting between two of his great
journeys a great sorrow fell on David. Mrs.
Livingstone, whom he loved the more the longer
he lived with her, died, and the man who had
faced so many deaths himself and braved so many
dangers without fear, broke down and wept like
a child. How lonely he must have felt, with his
dear children far away in England, as he buried
his beloved Ma-Robert under a baobab tree at
Shupanga! Mrs. Livingstone had been away in
Scotland looking after their children and always
anxious to be with her husband in his work in
Africa. She had only been with him a few months
when she was stricken with fever and despite all
that the Doctors did to keep her, she had died.
What a brave spirit David showed afterwards
when he said that although he was heartbroken
by her death he would keep a stiff upper lip and
carry on his work. "I am determined," he said
"that I will not swerve a hair's breadth from my
course."

VII

ACROSS THE OCEAN

DAVID had asked for a new vessel specially invented for river navigation to be sent out. This was built in such a way that it could be taken to pieces quite easily. Each piece was of a size that one man could carry on land, because there would be long stretches of the rivers and lakes which were not navigable, either because they were too shallow or because too much weed grew in the waters. When this new vessel which was called the *Lady Nyassa* was put together at Shupanga a large crowd of natives assembled to watch. Great was their surprise when this vessel of iron was successfully launched and a great cheer went up as she slipped easily and smoothly into the water.

The *Lady Nyassa* which had cost £6,000 was paid for by David himself from the money he had obtained from the sale of his book of "Missionary Travels" written when he was last home in England.

Unfortunately about this time both Charles Livingstone and Dr. Kirk became ill with fever and it became clear that they would have to go home to England, so disappointed because he could not go on with the expedition he returned with his friends to the coast. He was sad, too, because the British Government thought his mission had not been a success, and stopped sending any more money to pay for his travels. This led to him coming home again. But as if to show how plucky he was, he actually crossed the Indian Ocean from Africa to India in his little lake steamer *Lady Nyassa*. The real reason was that he was afraid that if he sold the ship in Africa she would fall into the hands of the slave-traders and be used for the traffic in human beings which he hated so much. But after braving all the dangers in Central Africa, David thought little of facing the perils of the ocean in a little cockle-shell of a steamer.

When we remember that the journey to Bombay was nearly two thousand five hundred miles and that he navigated the ship all the way by himself we realise what a fine feat of seamanship he achieved, in a vessel invented, not for the Indian Ocean, but for the lakes and rivers of Africa. The white men on board were too ill with fever to help with the running of the ship, so on top of his other responsibilities David had to instruct the crew of natives from the Zambezi country as well.

Livingstone had been looking forward to a long rest and for an opportunity to see something of his own family from whom he had been separated for so many years, but it was not to be. The reports that he had sent home about Lake Nyassa and reports from other explorers about Lake

Tanganyika had aroused the wide interest of many in England and it was not long after his arrival before he was visited by Sir Roderick Murchison who persuaded David to prepare for yet another expedition.

Reassuring David that he would look after his family while he was away, Sir Roderick helped him to make all the necessary preparations. Lord John Russell, thinking that David would be expecting some personal reward for all his labours, sent an ambassador to see him to see what honour could be conferred on him, but David, reassured by Sir Roderick's promise that his family would not be in want, would not ask for anything at all for himself, but added "If you stop the Portuguese slave trade you will gratify me beyond measure."

The Government uncertain about the success of this new expedition did not provide much money for it and only gave £500. An old college friend of David's gave £1,000 and about £2,000 was raised by public subscription. David gave all the money he earned from his new book written about this time on "The Zambezi and its Tributaries," together with £2,000 which he raised by the sale of the *Lady Nyassa* in Bombay. I mention all these figures so that you can see just how much David did himself to provide for the expedition. Alas, after he had gone into the African interior the Bank with which he had deposited his money was ruined and all David's money was lost!

It was fortunate that the Government had

appointed David as H.M.'s Consul to the tribes in the interior of Africa, for at least he could depend for some help on the resources of the British Government at a time when his own funds were almost nil.

This was to be David's last expedition and he was never to see England or his sons and daughters again. He knew that if Africa was ever to be a Christian land the slave trade must be stopped and though it might cost him his life he set out to end that trade.

David set off from England, sailed over to France and from there across the seas to Bombay where he had left his two African friends Chuma and Wekorani and with them and some Indian natives he sailed for Zanzibar. Soon the party were heading up the Rovuma into the heart of the jungle which extends along a plateau for many miles between two mountain ranges. Here the trees grew so closely together and the whole area was so completely overgrown with creepers that even in the day time it seemed dark, but they managed to hack their way through.

It was as they were going through this wild country that some of David's native servants deserted him and refused to take such a perilous journey. To cover up their desertion they spread a rumour that Dr. Livingstone had been murdered by a party of Mafite at a place called Mapunda. The rumour reached England, but although something of the dangers which David was facing every day was known to the people at home so

that no one would have been surprised that David
had been violently put to death, there were many
of his friends who refused to accept the report
until they had heard more details. Among these
friends was Sir Roderick Murchison who with
many others still hoped for news which would tell
them that David was alive.

The first gleam of hope came in a despatch
to the Foreign Office from Mr. Seward who
claimed to have spoken to various tribes who
had seen David after the date that the rumour
said he had died. Sir Roderick Murchison
encouraged by this report arranged with the
Government to cooperate with the Royal Geographical Society in an expedition to Lake Nyassa
which would settle the question of whether David
was still alive or not. This expedition sailed for
Africa and successfully navigated the Zambezi. In
a boat built to be carried in sections and assembled
on the spot, like Livingstone's *Lady Nyassa*,
they crossed the Lake after which that boat was
named and, meeting with Marenga the chief,
heard certain news that David was alive and had
been in touch with him only a little while before,
while some of his men had seen him even more
recently still going on further into the interior.
Marenga was also able to tell them that the
natives who had deserted David had been
questioned by him. They had admitted that they
did not relish exploring such dangerous places as
those in which he was travelling and therefore
they had gone home. "There is a limit to all

things," they had said. Fortunately for Africa and for the end of the slave trade there, David never recognised any such limits in his expeditions.

Sir Roderick's expedition although they had not seen David for themselves, returned to the Zambezi and home to England well satisfied that the rumour was groundless and that David was still very much alive.

David had by now penetrated far into the interior. From the Rovuma he had continued over the watershed above it.

VIII

HIS LAST MAJOR JOURNEY

AGAIN he reached the shores of Lake Nyassa,
seeing many slave-gangs on the way, and even the
skeletons and bodies of slaves who had died as
they were being hurried to the coast to be sold.
It was a terrible journey, through dank forests into
which the sunlight could not reach, across dreary
swamps, and over rough hills upon which the hot
sun beat pitilessly. Deluges of rain swept over
David and his men as they toiled along. They had
not much food, and the hard maize corn broke
their teeth. David became so thin that he said any
one could easily guess how much they could get
for his bones. A long year's hard journeying
brought him to the edge of a lake called Tanganyika. Then he pressed on, and discovered two
more great inland seas—Lakes Mweru and
Bangweolo—but now David was sick unto death,
and he had to rest to regain his strength.

Often Livingstone's patience was sorely tried
by his men—the natives who acted as his bearers.
On this last great journey to Ujiji, Livingstone
turned aside to discover Lake Bangweolo, but his
men rebelled. They wanted to go straight on to
Ujiji. All, excepting five, flatly refused to go with
him to the lake. Probably they had been in

contact with an Arab slave-trader who had corrupted their minds. Livingstone did not get angry when his men tried to upset his plans. He felt in his own mind that he could not blame them. They were sick of tramping day by day, carrying their loads. Livingstone was weary of it, too. So when they rebelled he did not scold, but quietly went his way without them. This gentleness must have touched their savage hearts, for on the way back they met Livingstone, and offered their services to him again. Always Livingstone made the utmost allowance for the other people's failures and misdeeds. He was concious of defects in himself, and that made him lenient to others. "I also have my weaknesses," he wrote.

Of all the great trials Livingstone had to endure, the worst perhaps came when he reached Ujiji, where he expected to find medicine and stores, and, above all, letters from home. It was the beginning of the year 1869. Livingstone had waded naked to the waist in Lake Bangweolo, where the leeches fastened themselves on his legs and had to be wrenched off. He had an illness lasting ten weeks, which enfeebled him so that he could not walk. A cough worried him by day and robbed him of sleep at night. The bearers carried him in a rude litter, but he was jolted about terribly. Without medicine or food fit for a sick man to eat, Livingstone's plight was terrible. Scarcely expecting to get there, he prayed that he might reach Ujiji. The hope of those letters from home stayed him, but he saw himself lying dead on the way. No wonder he lost count of the days of the week and the month. At last, after enduring agonies, he was rowed across Lake Tanganyika in a canoe to the eastern shore, and landed at Ujiji. But alas, the stores upon whose presence at Ujiji he had counted so confidently were not there. They had been plundered, first on the way from the coast, and then—what remained of them—at Ujiji. Only a few fragments were to be found. The medicine, so sorely needed, had been left behind, thirteen days' journey away, by the bearers. So had the cheese which would have nourished Livingstone in his exhaustion. There was nothing to do but to send to Zanzibar for some more, and sit down to await their arrival at Ujiji. Yet even in this plight David wrote to his daughter, saying that he had broken his teeth tearing at maize, and had "such an awful mouth" that "if you expect a kiss from me you must take it through a speaking trumpet."

IX

STANLEY

FOR two years no news of David had reached the outside world. People were uneasy. They thought he must be dead. At this time a newspaper reporter was sent out by the *New York Herald*. The story that the paper wanted was "Where is Livingstone?" Mr. Stanley, the man selected for this assignment did not sail direct to Africa, but he went first to India. Finally arriving at Zanzibar he commenced to make arrangements for his difficult journey inland. Two months later he was on his way in search of Livingstone "dead or alive," as his editor had told him.

Stanley, like David, needed a large number of porters. He was transporting food and medical supplies not only for his own journey, but also he carried with him many things which he knew Livingstone would be wanting. His long file of bearers consisted of one hundred and ninety-two men. Stanley soon came up against some of the difficulties which David had been facing in all his long journeys across Africa. It was heard that David had been in the region of Ujiji. Half way towards this place Stanley fell ill with fever. He was unconscious for two whole weeks. During all this time he kept hearing the voice of his editor repeating—"Find Livingstone! find Livingstone! find Livingstone!" This was a time of great strain for Stanley. He had come so far, but who could say whether there was still any trace of Livingstone? He might have been dead a long time, and all his African friends might be dead also, or scattered far from Ujiji.

We can easily imagine the despair that began to get hold of him, the temptation to say that it was proved that the man for whom he was looking was dead, that there were no signs to bring back to show the people at home. Just at this crucial time something happened. Remember, Stanley had been the only white man among thousands of black men in all his journey; he had for a change plenty of time on his hands, especially while he was ill. During this time he thought about his early days, about when he was a boy, about when he was a young man. He remembered that he had the habit of reading his Bible, that he used to go to Church, and he pulled out his Bible in the middle of the jungle where he lay recovering from his sickness. It was as he read the familiar passages that something happened to him. God spoke to him, in a way that God speaks to everyone who will stop to listen, and Stanley prayed for forgiveness that he had forgotten God all these years. He had come to Africa searching for David Livingstone but the first person he found was God.

This did not mean the end of his difficulties. The undergrowth was just as dense, the swamps just as treacherous, but it did mean that Stanley was given the strength to overcome all the troubles. He no longer gave in to the idea that had been buzzing in his head, to quit and go home. He write in his diary, "While I can walk I am going on, and I will not leave Africa without Livingstone."

Starting out again on their way to Ujiji the party came upon a lake. It was terribly hot, and the air was so damp that the handkerchief which Stanley continually wiped across his forehead was wringing wet. The lake looked very cool in the shade of the overhanging trees, and without hesitating any more Stanley took off his clothes and was just about to jump in when one of the bearers called to him. As he paused there in the very act of diving he saw something move. He had taken the dark object at the lake's edge to be a tree root, but when it moved he thought better of his swim . . . it was the snout of a huge crocodile!

These were not the only troubles that this now smaller band of travellers had to face. They came upon a battle. Some Arab slave-traders had tried to capture slaves from a tribe who lived in the country through which Stanley had to pass. When Stanley's party arrived the natives were getting the best of it, and the bearers soon joined in on their side, but unfortunately the Arabs came back at them with such force that the natives were scattered and Stanley nearly lost his life. Several of his men were killed, but the rest continued the exhausting march. Sometimes they showed signs of mutiny and Stanley had to pretend that he

would turn them over to the slavers, or that he
would shoot them as he did the wild beasts which
they cooked and ate on the way. This was the
only way in which he could keep them together,
but it was effective. When they were happy they
would sing, but when they were unhappy they
threatened to run away, which would certainly
have meant the death of Stanley. We have seen
already how David kept his men together, and how
devoted they were to him. It is interesting to
compare these two men in the way they treated
those who served them.

As they came to a village one morning, after
marching since dawn, a very excited native
rushed up to Stanley and said that there was a
white man in the village. The news was stagger-
ing, could Livingstone really be here? If it was not
Livingstone, who could it be? But it must be the
end of his search, no other white man had ever
been as far as this, surely this must be Livingstone?
In a few moments Stanley was shown to the hut
from which a pale face looked out, but a brief
glance showed that this was not Livingstone, it
was a native whose skin was paler than the rest,
in fact an albino, but he was not even a white
man at all. The great disappointment was hard
to bear. At one instant Stanley was full of ex-
pectancy, and in the next all his hopes had been
crushed. Taking courage he told his porters that
the search must go on.

Soon they arrived at another village where
some natives sat around resting. They were not

local men as even Stanley could see. They belonged to the tribe which had its home much
nearer to the coast, and when he asked them
what they were doing there the answer came,
"We are taking the supplies for the Doctor."
This then was the party which had left Zanzibar
several months before Stanley, and they appeared
to be quite happy to take a long rest half way. We
can imagine that Stanley gave them quite a
"rocket". He knew what the supplies would mean
to Livingstone, and how eagerly he would be
looking for his mail, the porters were no doubt
told to get on their way and quickly. Stanley took
with him in his own party the man who had been
carrying the precious letters from David's family
and friends at home, and left the others to follow
on.

A few days later at Ujiji, David's faithful African boy, Susi, ran to him crying: "An Englishman; I see him." David, a "mere ruckle of
bones," with his supplies at a very low ebb,
could not believe it, but in a few minutes Stanley
came forward, raising his hat. Words came easily
to the journalist as a rule, yet when he stood face
to face with Livingstone, the man for whom he
had been searching nearly a whole year, tears
came to his eyes and all he could say was, "Doctor
Livingstone, I presume!" The phrase with which
he might have greeted anyone in his office back
home in New York!

There were so many questions that David
wished to ask, so much had been happening in the

outside world about which he had heard nothing.
There was no radio network with news broad-
casts to keep him in touch with what was going
on. There was no telegraph service, no telephone,
no faster way of reaching him than the way
Stanley had come.

The two men shook hands. "I thank God,
Doctor, I have been permitted to see you," said
Stanley. "I feel thankful," replied David Livingstone, "that I am here to welcome you." This was
on 28th October, 1871. Stanley was just in time.
He brought David new life. For long months
Livingstone had not seen a white man or heard a
word spoken in the English language. Try to
imagine what these two men had to say to each
other. Stanley brought David home letters that
made his heart glad. He had news to tell of
Livingstone's children, and tidings of the outside
world, strange and thrilling for the lonely exile.
How they must have talked! They stayed
together until 14th March, 1872—over four
months.

During all this time Stanley watched with the
eye of a newspaperman the way in which
Livingstone went about his work. He was one of
only a very few who were able to watch him
caring for the Africans, giving them medicine,
advice, all sorts of help in various ways, beside
doing his most important work, preaching the
Gospel of his Master. We have cause to be thankful that Stanley was able to see all this for he has
written a book relating to us his experiences in

finding David, and his impressions of that great man. One day you may well read the "Autobiography of Henry M. Stanley."

On the morning after his arrival at Livingstone's camp Stanley woke up with a start. He thought he could hear a choir singing, and he rubbed his eyes and pinched himself to make sure that he was not still asleep. He was most certainly wide awake, but where did the sound of those fine deep voices come from? He had rarely heard such a wonderful chorus back home, but to hear a choir in the heart of Africa was the last thing that Stanley had expected. Now he recognized the music, it was a hymn he used to sing very often, and now it was being sung with a great deal of gusto: "Onward Christian Soldiers!"—came the chorus, and before he knew it almost, Stanley found himself joining in. All of a sudden it stopped. Livingstone came into the hut and apologised for waking Stanley so early. "It was our usual choir practice," he said, "I hope you were not disturbed by it." Every day after that Stanley was up in time to take part in the choir practice too, and while David swung his arms about with terrific enthusiasm keeping them in time, Stanley added his tenor to the lusty bass and resounding treble voices of the Africans.

The arrival of Stanley was made the occasion of a feast. The boys of the village were told to chase after the fatted pig, and a scramble began with the squealing pig evading them all the time until cornered against the wall of a hut. Then the cook took charge and started to make ready for the evening meal.

Meanwhile Stanley tried to answer the countless questions which David put to him. The letters from home had told him a lot of personal news which he was glad to have, but he had been for months with no newspaper, and a great many important events had been happening of which he was entirely ignorant. The two men talked at great length, and their discussion covered a very wide range of subjects.

At last the time came for the feast, and though he was not in the habit of eating much, Livingstone joined in the fun and enjoyed the welcome party in honour of his unexpected guest. The company of another white man was a real tonic to Livingstone, as he tells us in his own diary, and after his arrival they both had four meals a day in contrast to the two a day previously, and David's health improved as a result. It was soon a very healthy Livingstone who was able to set out on a voyage of exploration around the northern part of Lake Tanganyika.

Once more they needed many porters to carry the food, medicines, beads (which would buy them anything they wanted from the local people through whose country they might pass) and other necessaries such as a rifle to shoot lions or elephants if they should attack their party. It was always as well to be ready for that kind of an adventure ! This time there were also the sextant, compass and chronometer which David needed in his making of maps of this unknown part of the continent.

Each day readings would be taken and David would write them carefully in his note-book, then as he was able he made these readings into a map. This kind of map we call a "contour" map because it traces the "contours" or places which are at an equal height above sea level. David was at this time trying to establish where the source of the river Nile lay, and he thought it was near Lake Tanganyika. If you look at the map you will see how wrong he was about this, but that does not mean that his accurate and carefully noted observations were not valuable. From his maps the true structure of the hills of the region was first learnt.

Stanley now began to think about the journey home, and asked Livingstone when he would be ready to start out. The surprising reply came quickly, "I cannot leave Africa with my work unfinished."—"But surely my dear doctor you don't seriously think of staying here now that I have found you?"—"I was not lost, nor indeed was I hiding," answered David, who was surprised to learn that Stanley had supposed that he would be able to return to England. This announcement of David's did not please Stanley very much, as his editor, he knew, hoped that there would be an opportunity for an exclusive story from the pen of Livingstone, but that was not to be. The newspaper reporter would have to undertake that lengthy trek homeward on his

own just as he had come. Livingstone would
not leave Africa while there was strength in his
body, Stanley could see that, and after he became
feeble from the renewed attacks of fever which
were sure to come, he would die in the continent
for which he had worked so hard and so long.
Although he realised that it was useless Stanley
argued with David and tried to persuade him
to come home. "You're front page news you
know doctor!" he told him. "There would be
lecture tours and articles for you to write to
arouse interest in the work out here." David
was not a little surprised to hear that he was
"front page news," this provided a contrast to
the situation as he saw it while waiting for months
on end in the heart of the jungle for badly needed
supplies. There had been times when he was
refused things which were absolutely essential
for his work, and the difficulties caused in such a
way gave him much discouragement. Even to-day
there are times when those on the mission field are
hampered by lack of equipment, whether it is
Bibles or bandages, hospitals or helpers, pennies
or prayers.

The refinements of a modern hospital were
something about which Livingstone knew nothing,
and we are told of a minor operation which
he performed while Stanley was with him.
There arrived one day at David's hut a strong
native with a thorn in his foot. The thorn had
gone in very deep and the wound had turned
septic. It proved necessary to use a knife to

extract it properly. In those days there was no
ether or cocaine to ease the patient's suffering,
so Stanley had a part to play in this operation.
As David prepared the wound Stanley took hold
of the patient's arms to prevent him from
struggling. In a few moments the doctor removed
the troublesome thorn and the grateful native
went away with a bandage on his foot. It was a
frequent occurrence for the natives to be bothered
by thorns in this way as of course they never wore
shoes, and until the arrival of the doctor this
often meant a great deal of pain. Sometimes
even the wound might have been the cause of
death. David was not only concerned to heal
the disease which he found about him, but rather
as we have seen, he was anxious to show the
natives how Jesus cared for them. They would
come to David with their various troubles, what-
ever they might be, for they always found him
ready to help them, and always he seemed to
know the best way out of any difficult situation.

All this Stanley watched with great interest.
and we read something of the impression which
it made upon him. He said that you could take
any point in Livingstone's character and analyse
it carefully, and that he would challenge any
man to find a fault in it. "His gentleness never
forsook him," said Stanley, "and his hopefulness
never deserted him. No harassing anxieties,
distraction of mind, long separation from home
and kindred could make him complain. He
thought all would come out right at last, he had

such faith in the goodness of Providence. To the stern dictates of duty he sacrificed home and ease, the pleasures, refinements and luxuries of civilised life. His was the Spartan heroism, the inflexibility of the Roman, the enduring resolution of the Anglo-Saxon never to relinquish his work though his heart yearned for home, never to surrender his obligations till he could write 'Finis' to his work. In him," wrote Stanley, "religion exhibited its loveliest features ; it governed his conduct, not only towards his servants, but towards the natives, the bigoted Mohammedans, and all who came in contact with him. Without religion," wrote the newspaper reporter, "Livingstone, with his ardent temperament, his enthusiasm, his high spirit and courage, must have become uncompanionable and a hard master. Religion tamed him and made him a Christian gentleman ; the crude and wilful have been refined and subdued ; religion has made him the most companionable of men and indulgent of masters, a man whose society is pleasureable to a degree."

Now Stanley was to make ready for his return journey. Among the letters which he had brought for the doctor was one from his daughter in which she told her father that though she would very much like to see him she would be much happier to know that he was staying if he thought that was right. We may not be surprised at Livingstone's feeling great happiness at this display of real spirit by his daughter.

The day for the party to leave came at last and the doctor arranged to accompany them part of the way to Zanzibar and then to leave Stanley to go on alone. There was just one more occasion on which Stanley was to be glad of the presence of Livingstone, this wàs it.

As the bearers strode along under the loads the tall grasses almost hid the front of the column from David's view, and when they stopped dead in their tracks the reason for the hold up was not clear. Stanley came up to the front with Livingstone and they were faced by a very ferocious band of tribesmen who carried long blow pipes through which they could shoot very accurately with poisoned arrows. Livingstone wasted no time. If he had done nothing then the column might well have been wiped out ; he went up to them and told them that he was a white man who had never harmed a black; the result of his bravery was the more surprising to Stanley as it happened so quickly, all the natives disappeared back into the long grass from which they had come, and the party went on its way unmolested.

After a few days march from Ujiji Stanley told Livingstone with much regret that he thought that it was time for him to turn back.

The parting of these two men was full of good wishes that each might have a safe journey, Stanley to the coast to send back supplies to David, and David himself back into the heart of the continent to make maps and to open up the interior of Africa. Stanley perhaps knew in his heart that he would be the last white man to see David and it was all the more hard to say good-bye and leave him there so alone. Livingstone said good-bye with these words, "You have done what few men could do—far better than some great travellers I know—and I am grateful to you for what you have done for me. God guide you safe home and bless you, my friend. Farewell!"

When Stanley left David he still had many weary miles of swamp, jungle and disease-ridden country to cover. There were still hostile natives through whose country he must pass, and it was some months later that he arrived at Zanzibar. He arranged for the supplies to be sent to David, choosing men as his experience had taught him. He had begun to know the right sort of man to employ, for some of those whom he had chosen previously had not been much help, they had run off in ones and twos with what they had on their heads, or they had been quarrelsome. He sent his party on their way, and then set out for England with the news of Livingstone.

Some people thought he was not telling the truth, and it was heartbreaking after all the difficulties that he had encountered that Stanley should have to face such accusations of being a fraud. It was not possible to convince some of his critics that he was indeed speaking the truth until further news came from Africa to say that Livingstone's body had been brought to the coast by some of his African servants.

After Stanley went on his way to Zanzibar David had gone back to Ujiji to await the supplies which he promised to send. He had a long time to wait, six long months altogether, and this was a long time for David to be kept in one place. As soon as the supplies came through he set off again on a further exploration. But this was to be his last, for after many years in the heat and swamp David became weak, he found it difficult to walk, and had to ride on a donkey and at last had to be carried in a litter or stretcher. This was a sort of hammock tied onto a bamboo pole carried by two natives. They could not help swinging it to and fro as they went along, and so this was not quite so luxurious a form of travel as might be thought. By this time he was sixty years of age, and at sixty even men who have lived in ease at home soon get tired and feel illness much more than when they are young. Livingstone's life had been a terribly hard one—he had travelled 29,000 miles in Africa, and that is a long way. Now he was "knocked up quite," as he wrote in his diary. He had still the heart of a lion, and giving up did not enter into his thoughts. But on 29th April, thirteen months after saying goodbye to Stanley, he was carried into a village called Ilala, where his faithful black boys built a hut while drizzling rain fell. They laid him inside, and Susi kept watch at the door. Two mornings later Susi, looking inside, saw David on his knees as if he were praying. As he did not move, Susi went in to him; but David Livingstone was dead. Death had touched him gently as he prayed, and he had passed into a happier world to be with God and with Jesus whom he had loved and served so well.

Livingstone, I am sure, would have wished to die as he did; but I feel sorry that he did not know what happened to his body after his life passed away in Chetambo's village. Perhaps he did know. For those faithful black men, who were with him at the end, Susi and Chuma, showed their love for him in a wonderful fashion.

X

TO THE COAST

THE faithful servants first buried David's heart under a tree. His "heart" had always been in Africa, and they felt, I am sure rightly, that it should always stay there now that he was dead. There are many monuments in different places in commemoration of Livingstone, but none can be quite as full of meaning as the place where that tree stood. Indeed, perhaps it is still there to-day.

When they had roughly embalmed David's body they wrapped it very carefully in a cloth, and tied their precious load to a bamboo pole, as they had done his hammock when he was too ill to walk, and a small band of them set off for the coast. It was a distance of 1,500 miles, three times as far as from Brighton to Inverness ! ! As we have already realised the country was not so easy to cover either, and the intrepid party no doubt started out with a prayer, as well as a great deal of faith and devotion, in their hearts.

They had been on their way only a little while when troubles came upon them. The swamps through which they had to pass were always inclined to give them fever, for the tsetse flies are more numerous and therefore more

effective over swampy country. Fever struck
them again and again as well as a more serious
complaint; this was a form of rheumatism,
which only old people suffer from as a rule, very
painful for all of them. With so many miles to
cover they could not hope to get very far if their
speed was greatly reduced by such an illness,
but far from getting depressed and giving up they
struggled on until they came to higher ground.

Even having crossed the swamp their difficulties were not ended. They still had to cross the
Luapula. This river was four miles wide at the
point at which they had to cross it, four miles up
to their waists in the strong current in which
crocodiles were always to be found. Happily
there were no hungry crocodiles on that particular day and the party crossed in safety.

Taking a short rest after crossing the river
there was time to dry in the boiling sun. As
they began to move again they felt hostile eyes
watching them. It did not take them long
to discover that the local inhabitants were not
pleased to see them, and a spear narrowly missed
the first man in the column as if to tell them that
they had better not come any further. But these
devoted servants of David had not come so far
just to be scared away with a few arrows, and they
went steadily on. The way was immediately
barred by a ferocious band of warriors who
demanded to know who it was that they were
carrying in the cloth. It seemed that the news
of their journey had gone before them, and the

faithful band had to pretend to turn back or they would have all been killed. They decided that it would be quite impossible to travel through this particular territory with the body so obviously to be seen. A little scheme was planned. A reel of cloth was done up in imitation of the one in which Livingstone's body was being carried, a few of them then went on in a direct route with this bundle. When the hostile natives saw that it was only cloth which they were carrying they were allowed to pass. Meanwhile the actual body was carried by the rest of the small band by a devious route which avoided the villages. Expert in the knowledge of the forest and how to move about it without making much noise, they rejoined the decoy party later on when they were well clear of the interfering natives. The reason why the local people did not want the body of Livingstone to be brought across their land was their fear that it would bring them bad luck. Everything to these simple Africans could be made acceptable or otherwise according as to whether the witch-doctor said that it meant good luck or bad. Once this had been decided by the witch-doctor it was very difficult indeed to convince the people that there was no truth in what they had been told. David spent a great deal of time in doing this, sometimes it could be done quickly. For instance the case when he used a burning glass to make the grass catch fire, this at once gained for him the confidence of the natives who, the moment before, had wanted to spear him to death because their witch-doctor had told them that he brought bad luck.

A little further on they came into more hostile bands, but these did not mind what they were carrying, they just attacked them and the small and weary band had to fight back as best they could. It was certainly a one-sided battle, but they were equipped with rifles, and this probably did more than anything else to frighten the attackers away.

They came upon a party of white men. These had been sent out by the Royal Geographical Society for which society David had been doing some of his work of exploration. The white men knowing something of the difficulties of travel under any circumstances through the forests and swamps, were amazed at the courage of this band of Africans who had already come some hundreds of miles on their way to the coast with the body of Livingstone. It was proposed to them that they should bury the body there where the two parties had met, but the Africans would not hear of it. They had so far been given the strength to carry on, and their determination was no less than when they had started out.

There were still more natives who had heard about the party bringing the body of Livingstone to the coast. They wanted to make them pay in cloth, in "valuables" such as mirrors and beads, and in anything which the small party had with them, for the privilege of carrying the body through their country. They were caused much delay on account of this, and so another scheme was thought of to make the journey easier. It was spread abroad that Livingstone had been buried and the body was again wrapped in cloth to disguise it from curious eyes, and since news travels fast in Africa through the beat of the tom-tom it was soon proclaimed throughout the country lying between them and the coast that the body of David was no longer on its way, but had been buried. This scheme was very helpful since nobody doubted that it was just a bale of cloth that they were now carrying.

The story has been told of how on this last stage of the journey to the coast a large snake appeared suddenly from the dense undergrowth. It went with speed straight at a little girl who was walking with them carrying a water-pot. The deadly sting struck her like a sharp knife and in a few moments she collapsed and having been carried for only a little way she died. The snake must have been a particularly vicious one as the story goes on to relate that a party of Arabs were passing the same place a little later, and exactly the same thing occurred. They hardly had time to notice what was wrong with the one who had been stung before he too fell down dead. They saw the little grave in which the girl had been laid and buried the dead Arab beside her.

Finally they reached Bagamoio on the coast. Here they gave the body over to the charge of the representatives of the British government. There was not much fuss made about it, and nobody there seems to have thought of the immense effort which went into the transporting of David's body all that way. One man, however, did realise something of what they had done, and paid for three of the faithful natives to come to London to pay their last respects to their beloved leader.

EPILOGUE

BROUGHT by a liner back home to England the
body of Livingstone was laid to rest in Westmin-
ster Abbey during a great funeral service, at
which the three African followers were present.
When you go next to the Abbey you can see the
black marble stone which marks the place where
he was buried. On it are these words, which
commemorate also the heroic journey under-
taken by the faithful natives :

BROUGHT BY FAITHFUL HANDS
OVER LAND AND SEA,
HERE RESTS
DAVID LIVINGSTONE
MISSIONARY,
TRAVELLER,
PHILANTHROPIST,
BORN MARCH 19TH, 1813
AT BLANTYRE, LANARKSHIRE,
DIED MAY 4TH, 1873
AT CHETAMBO'S VILLAGE, ULALA.

For thirty years his life was spent in an
unwearied effort to evangelize the native races, to
explore the undiscovered secrets, and abolish the

desolating slave trade of Central Africa, where with his last words he wrote :

> " All I can say in my solitude is, may Heaven's rich blessing come down on every one—American, English or Turk —who will help to heal this open sore of the world."

Along the right border of the stone are the words :

> TANTUS AMOR VERI, NIHIL EST QUOD NOSCERE MALIM, QUAM FLUVII CAUSAS PER SAECULA TANTA LATENTES.

And along the left border :

> OTHER SHEEP HAVE I WHICH ARE NOT OF THIS FOLD ; THEM ALSO MUST I BRING, AND THEY SHALL HEAR MY VOICE.

A few of the things David Livingstone said are so fine that they are worth learning by heart. Here are some of them:

"Fear God and work hard."

"I can be rich without money."

"A life of selfishness is one of misery."

"Be manly Christians and never do a mean thing."

"Depend upon it, a kind word or deed is never lost."

"I shall not swerve a hairbreadth from my work while life is spared."

"Science and Religion are not hostile but friendly to each other."

"One of the discoveries I have made is that

there are vast numbers of good people in the world."

"I view the end of the geographical feat as the beginning of the missionary enterprise."

"Nothing earthly will make me give up my work in despair. I encourage myself in the Lord my God, and go forward."

"Good works gain the approbation of the world, and though there is antipathy in the human heart to the Gospel of Christ, yet when Christians make their good work shine all admire them."

A very tender heart beat in David Livingstone's breast. On one of his great journeys he had among his companions a poodle which he called Chitane. Livingstone was very fond of this faithful dog, which he said had more pluck than a hundred country dogs. Chitane took charge of the whole line of march during the journeyings. He would run to see the first of the line of black carriers, then back to the last carrier, barking at him by way of telling him to hurry up. When the line stopped Chitane would find out which hut Livingstone occupied, and would not let a country cur come in sight of it. He never stole himself, and did not let other dogs steal. In crossing a marsh a mile wide and waist-deep, Livingstone's pet came to a sad end. "I went over first," wrote Livingstone, "and forgot to give directions about the dog, and all were too much engaged in keeping their balance to notice that he swam among them till he died." Livingstone's

grief over poor Chitane's death was very real.
At the time he was himself very ill through
having to live on maize, millet porridge, and
mushrooms. "But," he added, always ready to
be quite cheerful if there is but the smallest
warrant for it, "we got a cow yesterday, and I am
to get milk to-morrow."

I have given you a very poor idea of the real
hero Livingstone was, if I have not made it clear
that he did nearly all his great work in the teeth
of almost heart-breaking disappointments. You
know what it is, perhaps, to want to do something
very much indeed, and to find all kinds of
obstacles in the way. Now Livingstone was trying
to do gigantic things—to open Africa to the
Gospel and to commerce, to end the slave trade,
and to solve big problems in geography and
science. And at every stage in his efforts he got
rebuffs. First the Missionary Society directors did
not quite share his idea that before Central
Africa could be evangelised it must be explored,
and that he was the man to explore it. Then
some of the white missionaries were jealous of
him, and made his task harder, though they saw
their mistake later and were proud of their
great leader. Then Mrs. Livingstone died and
left her husband lonely, and with his little
motherless children far away. Wherever he went
in Africa he found horrors and tragedies which
he vainly tried to cure. When the British
Government entrusted him with an exploring
mission it had not patience to see it through, and

stopped sending money to pay the cost. Troubles met him at every turn. Delays upset his plans. Worries almost drove him mad. He suffered thirst and hunger. Fever and dysentery laid him low. Always he ran the risk of being killed by hostile natives or by sly slave-dealers. His stores got lost or stolen. His papers sank in a wrecked ship. His journeys through dense forests and over trackless deserts wore him down. His supplies of clothing ran short. Time and time again he just escaped death by accidents to canoes. Wild beasts made his life unsafe. Guides failed him. Savage chiefs denied him passage through their country. He went months at a time without a letter from home, or a glimpse of a white face. Yet he bore all this, and if you read his journal you will find that while now and again he was downhearted, he was generally cheerful and always brave. He lived very close to his God. His Bible was his greatest solace. He felt daily the companionship of Jesus Christ even when he was most solitary.

Do not run away with the idea that David Livingstone was a great giant of a man to whom all this labour was light work. He was a man of middle height—about five feet six inches high—and he was of slender build. It was not bodily strength, but power of will, that carried him along, and made him able to trudge along, day after day, with that "forward tread, firm, simple, resolute, neither fast nor slow, no hurry and no dawdle." Livingstone lived his life and did his work fired by a great ideal. He believed that God

Himself had called him to open Africa; and having opened it he left it to others, under God's guidance, to take up the task where he laid it down

. . . . .

When people write a letter, they often add something after the signature to what they have written. That is called a postscript. And I want to add a postscript to this story. David Livingstone has been dead now over 80 years; but his name is honoured and his fame is ever fresh, because he lived nobly and died nobly, and because he led a great crusade in a way which made other brave men come forward to see that it was carried on. There are lots of missionaries who are working in the Mission Field because of David Livingstone. Africa is dotted all over with Mission stations, and, just as David Livingstone believed, the Gospel of Jesus Christ fast destroyed the slave trade. And this was due to Livingstone, whose deathless story I have tried so to tell that you may love him; but most of all so that you may love the same Lord Jesus who made David Livingstone the hero that he was.

HEROES OF THE CROSS

LORD TONYPANDY

Catherine Swift

Lord Tonypandy is one of two new titles in the HEROES OF THE CROSS series. George Thomas became a favourite household name as the former Speaker of the House of Commons, an office he filled between 1976 and 1983. During his time as Speaker, he had to deal with a stormy parliament, as well as taking a leading part in the Queen's Silver Jubilee celebrations and the marriage of the Prince and Princess of Wales. The rich privileges which belonged to him as Speaker were a far cry from the poverty he had known during his childhood in the South Wales valleys.

But his role as Speaker was only the crowning achievement of a very full and active Christian life. George Thomas was born into a Methodist family, and he regularly preached in chapels and churches everywhere. During the 1950s and 60s, he preached in almost every large town and city in Britain. He was also a Christian socialist, elected as a Labour MP in the first General Election after World War II. His kindness and hard work on behalf of his constituents left a lasting mark on many people's lives.

This new biography, written specifically for young readers, perfectly captures the warm-hearted human spirit and the towering Christian witness of one of Britain's most loved national figures.

Pocket paperback 0551 02029-6

HELEN KELLER
Catherine Swift

Helen Keller is the latest title in the popular HEROES
OF THE CROSS series. Helen, the daughter of an
American Confederate army captain, was an intelligent
and lively child, until at the age of seventeen months a
severe illness struck. The illness left her totally blind
and deaf. Helen was spoiled by her parents and grew up
as an uncontrollable child. It was only when Annie
Sullivan arrived at the house and began to teach her
that she developed and grew in her understanding.

Through Annie, Helen eventually learned how to
communicate with the outside world, and how to speak.
She went on to devote her life to working on behalf of
blind and deaf people. She founded the American
Foundation for the Blind and travelled the world many
times, making extensive lecture tours. She was
sustained in her work by Annie, who remained her
lifelong companion, and by her strong faith in God.

Catherine Swift's new biography opens up the inspiring
story of Helen's life for young readers. Vividly told,
Helen Keller is a story that will keep every reader turning
the pages.

Pocket paperback 0551 02028-8